Getting To Know...

Nature's Children

POLAR BEARS

Caroline Greenland

Facts in Brief

Classification of the Polar Bear

      Class: *Mammalia* (mammals)

      Order: *Carnivora* (meat-eaters)

      Family: *Ursidae* (bear family)

      Genus: *Ursus*

      Species: *Ursus maritimus*

World distribution. Polar Bears live in all lands bordering on the Arctic Ocean.

Habitat. Mainly coastal areas; may move somewhat inland in summer and may winter on ice floes.

Distinctive physical characteristics. Thick creamy-white fur; relatively small head and ears; fur on the soles of its feet.

Habits. Solitary except in mating season; excellent swimmer and hunter; often wanders great distances in search of food.

Diet. Sea animals, including fish, walruses, and especially, seals; some grasses and berries in summer.

Canadian Cataloguing in Publication Data

Greenland, Caroline.
  Polar bears

(Getting to know—nature's children)
Includes index.
ISBN 0-7172-1944-5

1. Polar bears—Juvenile literature.
I. Title. II. Series.

QL737.C27G73 1985   j599.74'446   C85-098728-8

Have you ever wondered . . .

Do you know which large animal of the North is also known as Nanook, Ice King and Ice Bear? If you guessed the Polar Bear, you are right!

Most people have never seen a Polar Bear, except in a zoo. But its nicknames give you a hint about where you would find one in the wild. These huge white bears are only found where there is lots of ice and snow—in the far North.

Few animals could survive the winters of the Far North. But Polar Bears are well adapted to living in the cold. In fact, if there were such an event as a cold-weather olympics, this hardy bear would probably be in the finals for keeping warm, hunting and perhaps even swimming. Not bad!

Let's find out more about these champions of northern survival.

Into the Icy Water

Imagine how surprised a baby Polar Bear must be when it sticks its paw into the icy cold arctic water for the first time. Brrr!

Because Polar Bears sometimes have to swim to hunt, it is important for a Polar Bear cub to learn to swim. But ...oh... that water is cold!

To get her cubs into the water, a mother Polar Bear flops in first and swims a short distance away. The young cubs look nervous and whimper uncertainly. Finally one of them bellyflops in and swims to its mother. The second cub is not far behind.

Once the cubs have been in the water for a few minutes, they seem to start enjoying themselves. Soon they will be as much at ease in the water as their mother.

"You're sure I'll like it once I'm in?"

Polar Bear Relatives

What do weasels, raccoons, dogs and bears have in common? They are all distant relatives. But the Polar Bear's closest relatives are the Black and Brown Bears.

Black Bear

The Polar Bear is bigger than most of its relatives. Some huge male Polar Bears weigh as much as a compact car. That is a lot of bear! An average-sized male would tip the scales at 500 kilograms (1100 pounds). The females are considerably smaller.

A female Polar Bear is also called a sow. A male Polar Bear is called a boar.

Grizzly Bear

Polar Bear

If you were standing beside this bear, your head might just about reach his paw. A full-grown male bear can be well over 3 metres tall.

Polar Bear Country

Imagine visiting a place where there are no trees or grass, only ice and snow. It is dark, even though it is the middle of the day. An icy wind seems to cut right through your clothes. You look at a thermometer and notice that the temperature is far below freezing. Are you starting to get the chills?

You have just taken an imaginary trip to Polar Bear country in the winter. Polar Bears live in the lands surrounding the Arctic Ocean, the body of water that covers the North Pole. Because their main food is seal, they spend much of their time near the coast where the seals live.

In the summer the Arctic is a very different place. The snow and ice melt, and the land is covered with many kinds of plants and colorful flowers. During the summer some Polar Bears move inland and feast on plants, berries and small animals, but most follow the seals as they travel even farther North in search of fish.

Later, as winter approaches again, the seals and Polar Bears migrate back to their more southerly homes.

Opposite page:

It may look like cold, icy countryside to us, but to a Polar Bear, it's home.

Cold Weather Comfort

You might think this Polar Bear is wearing only one fur coat, but it is actually wearing two. It has a thick, short coat of underhair next to its skin to trap body-warmed air. Covering this is a longer outer coat of shining coarse guard hairs, which repel water, ice and snow like a raincoat. When a Polar Bear comes out of the water, it shakes itself off like a huge furry dog to rid its coat of icy water.

Under the skin is a layer of fat up to nine centimetres (3.5 inches) thick, which acts as insulation to keep the cold out.

No Cold Toes

Have you ever noticed how your hands, feet, ears and nose are the first parts of your body to get cold when you are playing outdoors on a frosty winter day? Well, animals are just like you. They feel the cold in those parts of their bodies too, especially in their ears. But Polar Bears' furry ears are very small and this means they lose less heat into the frosty air. And to keep its feet warm, the Polar Bear has a thick covering of fur on the soles of its feet. These built-in slippers also keep the bear from skidding on the ice.

Front paw

Rear paw

Those short, furry ears let less heat escape than long ones do.

15

Keeping Cool

The Polar Bear's cold-weather outfit keeps it
comfortable and warm—sometimes *too* warm.
In the summer, the Polar Bear sheds its heavy
winter coat, but even so it sometimes has a
problem cooling off. A hot bear solves this
problem by digging itself a summer den. It digs
deep into the ground, down to where the soil is
still frozen. As its body heat melts the frozen
ground, the bear digs down a little deeper. The
bear uses this "bear refrigerator" whenever it
needs to cool off.

*A Polar Bear's white coat makes it very
visible against the summer landscape.
Fortunately the bear has few enemies
and so little need to worry about being
spotted.*

Walk Like a Bear

Try walking on all fours by placing your hands and feet flat on the ground at each step. Point your fingers and toes slightly inward rather than straight ahead. How did you do?

It might not be easy for you, but a Polar Bear can get around just fine with this flat-footed, pigeon-toed walk. A Polar Bear often covers a large hunting territory in a day with its rather clumsy looking, ambling walk. It can even gallop quite fast for a short distance if it needs to.

They may walk slowly, but Polar Bears can cover a lot of kilometres in a day, and they can run very fast when they need to.

A Bear Slide

The ice and snow-covered land where the Polar Bear lives is mostly flat. But sometimes miniature mountains of ice and snow form. The Polar Bear can easily climb up these snow mountains, but getting back down is a problem.

Polar Bears have come up with two tricks to help them get downhill. One is to walk slowly using their front legs as brakes. The other is simply to lie down and slide on their bellies, headfirst. Sounds like fun, doesn't it?

Web-footed Super Swimmers

In snow, the Polar Bear's wide feet act like snowshoes and keep it on top of the snow. The bear's front feet are slightly webbed, like a duck's, and they make excellent swimming flippers. Polar Bears would not win any ribbons for speed swimming, but they might win a swimming marathon. They can dog-paddle for over 100 kilometres (60 miles) at one stretch if necessary! Their streamlined body, which is narrower in the front than the back, cuts easily through the water, a bit like the bow of a boat. Only the front feet are used when swimming; the back feet steer.

Long distance swimmer.

Underwater Swimmer

Sometimes the bear dives under the water to chase a seal or avoid a chunk of floating ice. It does not have to worry about getting water up its nose though. Polar Bears can close their nostrils as tightly as if they were wearing noseplugs. And they can hold their breath to stay underwater for as long as two minutes.

Polar Bears are at home in the water. Next time you visit the zoo, watch the Polar Bears swimming in their pool. With all that splashing and diving, they seem to be enjoying their swim.

Coming up for air.

Sharp Eyes, Sharp Nose

Polar Bears have good eyesight, which helps
them while hunting. They often stand up on
their hind legs to get a better view of what is
going on around them. The Polar Bear's sense
of smell is also excellent. It can help the bear
locate seals and other animals a great distance
away.

A good sense of sight and smell is important
for a Polar Bear because it lives in a cold barren
land where food is scarce most of the year. A
Polar Bear cannot afford to miss food, so its
eyes and ears must be keen.

Northern Hunters

Because the Polar Bear needs to eat an average
of four kilograms (9 pounds) of meat a day, it
must spend a lot of time hunting. Seals are the
Polar Bear's favorite food, but seals are not easy
to catch. They are fast-moving, clever and
cautious. To catch enough seals to survive, the
Polar Bear has come up with some unusual
hunting methods.

"Now that smells interesting . . . "

In winter seals hunt for fish by swimming under the ice. To catch a seal, a Polar Bear will wait patiently near one of the holes in the ice where seals come up to breathe. The bear knows that if it waits long enough a swimming seal will poke its head up through this breathing hole to take a gulp of air. When this happens, the Polar Bear tries to grab the seal. If it misses the seal, it will often move to a new hole and begin its long wait all over again.

Another hunting trick is to watch for a seal sunning itself on the ice. When it spots one, the bear crouches down low to the ground and begins to creep slowly up on the unsuspecting seal. Its white coat makes it difficult to see, and it also takes advantage of any big ice chunks or bumps in the ground to hide behind. When it is close enough to surprise the seal, it pounces!

A Polar Bear may also swim quietly up to seals dozing on an ice floe and leap out of the water onto them. This difficult feat seems to pose no problem for the powerful Polar Bear.

Keep Your Distance

Because of its size and strength, the Polar Bear has few enemies. However, it must watch out for walruses and Killer Whales—and other Polar Bears.

Bears usually avoid each other's company, so they seldom get close enough to fight. In fact when two bears have to pass by each other on the ice, they keep a distance equal to the length of a football field between them. Now that's not exactly friendly!

During the summer mating season, male Polar Bears may hurt or even kill each other when arguing about who is going to be a female's mate.

On the alert!

31

Starting a Family

When a female Polar Bear is four or five years old, she is ready to have a family. From late March to early June, she is approached by many males, but she only mates with the largest and strongest.

The couple stays together for days or even weeks. This is the only time male and female Polar Bears are found together.

Whichever of these males wins the fight will also win the female.

A Warm, Cozy Den

By mid-October the sow begins her search for a place to dig a den. She seems to know that the arctic winds will soon be howling and that she must find a warm place to have her babies.

She looks for a hill that faces south and is covered with plenty of snow. Here she digs out a den about the size of a bedroom but only one metre (3 feet) high. The den is higher than the entrance hole so that water from melting snow runs out of the den and warm air, which rises, does not escape. The den never gets toasty warm, but it *is* usually warmer than the frosty air outside.

Sometimes, if the weather turns bitterly cold, male Polar Bears may take shelter in a quickly dug den, but they never enter a den occupied by another bear. But most of the winter they wander in search of food and even sleep outdoors.

Between November and early January, the mother gives birth. Most often she will have two cubs, but sometimes only one or as many as four.

Opposite page:

Male Polar Bears rarely bother with a den unless the weather is especially bitter.

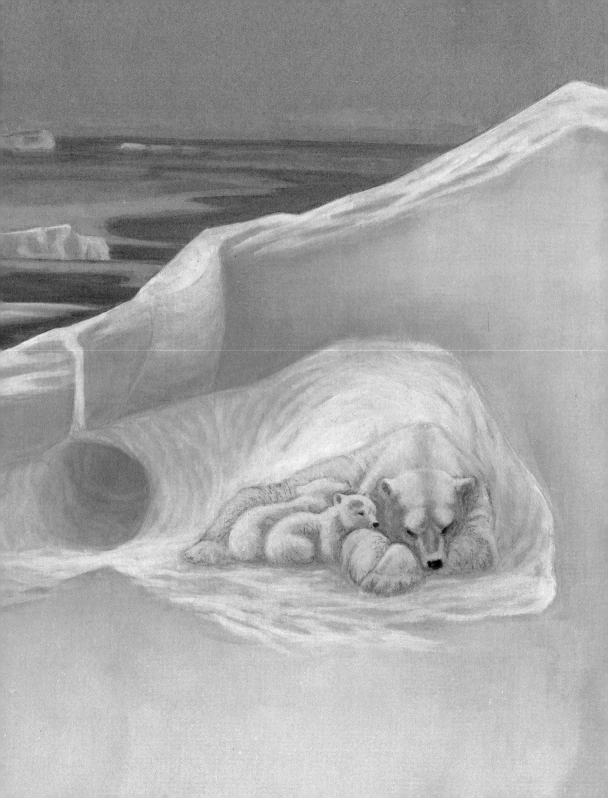

Bear Babies

How tiny and helpless the cubs are when they are born! Their huge mother must take care that she does not crush them by accident. The newborn cubs are hairless and deaf, and they are only about the size of guinea pigs. Their eyes do not open until they are at least two weeks old, and they spend the first two months of their lives in the warm den with their mother. During this period they nurse on their mother's milk and grow quickly.

By March, the cubs have a white woolly coat and weigh about 10 kilograms (22 pounds). Now mother and cubs are ready to leave the protection of their winter home for short hunting trips to the sea. The female is very hungry because she has not eaten all the time she was in the den—she lived on the fat of her body.

A Polar Bear shower. When they come out of the water, Polar Bears shake the wetness off their coats like big, furry dogs.

Hunting and Swimming Lessons

While their mother catches seals, the Polar Bear cubs stay close by and watch her carefully. Although they will still nurse for some time, they eventually must catch seals for themselves. By watching their mother, the cubs learn how to sneak up on seals and other important hunting skills.

The mother Polar Bear also encourages her cubs to practice swimming. Soon they are at home in the icy water. While the cubs are going through this learning stage, the Inuit call them "ah tik tok" which means "those that go down to the sea."

The sow will have her babies about 8 months after mating. She will usually only have cubs every 3 years.

Furry Hitchhikers

The sow is a good mother. While traveling across the snow and ice, she often lies down to allow her little ones to nurse or climb up on her to warm their feet. Or, if they grow tired while swimming, she lets them climb up on her back, piggy-back style. Sometimes young cubs have been seen hitching a ride by grabbing onto their mother's tail with their mouths.

The Cubs Grow Up

By the time the cubs are a year old, they have grown to about the size of a St. Bernard dog. But they still need their mother to protect them from wolves and adult Polar Bears. They will stay with their mother until they are one and a half years old or even older before starting life on their own.

To us a young Polar Bear's first few years on its own may seem like a cold and lonely life. It wanders by itself in the frozen North, rarely even seeing another Polar Bear. But Polar Bears prefer to live alone. They seem to enjoy wandering through the snowy arctic world. If they have learned their hunting skills well, they may live to be 20 to 30 years old and have several families of their own.

Special Words

Boar The male of various kinds of animals, including the Polar Bear.

Den Animal home.

Guard hairs Long coarse hairs that make up the outer layer of the Polar Bear's coat.

Ice floe Very large pieces of floating ice.

Insulation A material, such as fur or fat, that helps an animal keep heat in when it is cold.

Mate To come together to produce young.

Mating season Time of year when animals mate.

Nursing The drinking of milk from a mother's body.

Predator Animal that lives by hunting others for food.

Prey Animals that are food for predators.

Sow The female of various animals, including the Polar Bear.

INDEX

Cover Photo: Wayne Lankinen (Valan Photos)

Photo Credits: Wayne Lankinen (Valan Photos), pages 4, 9, 13, 17, 20, 26, 32-33, 34, 45; William Lowry (Lowry Photo), page 7; Stephen J. Krasemann (Valan Photos), page 10; Bill Ivy, pages 14, 30; Frank E. Johnson (Valan Photos), page 19; J.D. Taylor (Miller Services), page 23; J.A. Wilkinson (Valan Photos), page 24; B. Lyon (Valan Photos), page 29; R. Redhead (Network Stock Photo File), page 39; Dr. A. Farquhar (Valan Photos), page 41; R. Popko (Network Stock Photo File), page 42.

Getting To Know...

Nature's Children

SKUNKS

Laima Dingwall

Grolier

Facts in Brief

Classification of the Striped Skunk

Class: *Mammalia* (mammals)
Order: *Carnivora* (meat-eaters)
Family: *Mustelidae* (weasel family)
Genus: *Mephitis* (terrible smell)
Species: *Mephitis mephitis*

World distribution. Exclusive to North America. Closely related species found in various areas of North, Central, and South America.

Habitat. Areas of mixed forest and grassland are the preferred habitat, but the Striped Skunk is very adaptable, and can even be found in densely populated areas.

Distinctive physical characteristics. Shiny black fur with white stripe on face and two down the back; foul-smelling musk that can be sprayed; long straight claws suited for digging.

Habits. Active mainly at night; sprays its musk when angered or threatened; in the North, spends most of the winter inside den, but is not a true hibernator.

Canadian Cataloguing in Publication Data

Dingwall, Laima, 1953-
  Skunks

(Getting to know—nature's children)
Includes index.
ISBN 0-7172-1942-9

1. Skunks—Juvenile literature.
I. Title. II. Series.

QL737.C25D56 1985   j599.74'447   C85-098737-7

Have you ever wondered . . .

If you saw these cute and cuddly balls of black-and-white fluff you might want to pick them up and hug them. But watch out! These eight-week-old babies are skunks. They may be small, but their smell is mighty.

But there is more to skunks than their foul odor. Skunks are handsome, mild-mannered animals. And, believe it or not, they prefer to be left alone and not cause such a big stink!

These handsome black and white skunks are easy to spot in the grassy field.

Skunk Country

Wherever you live in North America you probably don't live far from one kind of skunk or another. Some skunks make their home in deserts, others in forests and along river valleys. Many live on farmland, where there is lots of food available.

You might even find some skunks in city backyards. If you do, treat them with respect. Remember the skunk may look harmless, but its spray is powerful.

Opposite page:

Where Skunks live in North America

Skunks, Skunks . . .

Four different kinds of skunks live in North America: the Hog-nosed, the Hooded, the Spotted and the Striped Skunk.

Hog-nosed Skunks live in the southwestern United States. They got their name because of—what else—their hog-like noses. They use these wide hairless snouts much like a pig does, to root or dig out food from the ground.

Scientists know very little about the Hooded Skunk that lives in the deserts of the southwestern United States. But they do know that it has the longest tail of all skunks—up to 38 centimetres (15 inches)—and has very long hair around its neck. This long hair looks rather like a hood—so now you know how the Hooded Skunk got its name!

The spots on the Spotted Skunks are really wavy broken-up stripes.

And More Skunks

Spotted Skunks, which live in most of the United States and parts of Canada, are the smallest of all the skunks and the only tree climbers. They have an unusual way of spraying enemies. Instead of just lifting their tails, they do a handstand on their front feet and let the spray fly over their backs.

The most common skunk of all is the Striped Skunk, which lives in most parts of North America. Striped Skunks are about the size of housecats, except they have short, stubby legs. Let's take a closer look at these well-known skunks.

Striped Skunk

Spotted Skunk

One Big Happy Family

The scientific name for the Striped Skunk is *Mephitis mephitis*. This is Latin for "terrible" smell, terrible smell."

Early North American settlers called the skunk "polecat" because it reminded them of a small, furry animal that lives in Europe. Even today many people call the skunk by this name.

It is not surprising that people get the skunk and the polecat mixed up. They both belong to the weasel family. Other North American weasels include the River Otter, Sea Otter, mink, fisher, ermine and wolverine.

Weasels come in all sorts of sizes and colors, but they all have one thing in common. They all produce strong-smelling musk in glands at the base of their tail. Can you guess which weasel makes the worst smell of all? If you answered the skunk, you are right.

Sniff Sniff

How would you describe the smell of a skunk's spray? One naturalist said it smelled like strong ammonia, garlic, burning sulphur, sewer gas and perfume musk all mixed up together. Pheww!

A skunk's spray smells so bad that it makes some people and animals sick. If it is sprayed on skin or eyes, it stings and burns. It may even cause temporary blindness for a few minutes. Even though the unpleasant effects of being sprayed by a skunk do not last long, animals learn from experience to stay away from a skunk when its tail goes up.

This Striped Skunk is ready to spray. It's easy to tell because its tail is straight up.

Warning Signals

A skunk does not spray its foul-smelling musk on every animal or person that it meets. Its glands only hold about one tablespoon of musk—enough for five or six sprays a week. So the skunk wants to save it for real emergencies.

Even if an enemy gets too close and the skunk becomes frightened or annoyed, it still does not automatically spray. Usually it will warn its enemy first. How? It lowers its head and hisses and growls. Then it stamps its front feet one at a time and rakes the ground with its long claws like a miniature bull. Finally it waves its bushy tail in warning.

This hole among the rocks makes a cozy den for the Striped Skunk.

Ready, Steady, Spray

If all its warnings do not scare the enemy away, the skunk gets ready to spray. It arches its back, lifts its tail and bends its body sideways so that its head and tail both point toward the enemy. Then—squirt!—it lets its spray fly from its tail glands.

When the skunk fires its spray, it lifts its tail high to keep the scent off its own fur. Other animals are not so lucky. A skunk can score a direct hit with its spray a car's length away. Once the spray is in the air, it breaks up into a fine mist that sticks and clings to fur and clothing. This smelly mist can spread downwind for over three-quarters of a kilometre (half a mile). And the smell can linger for hours.

Click. Click. Click. Baby skunks make clicking sounds with their tongues. As they grow older they start to squeal like a mouse.

Enemy List

It is not surprising that Striped Skunks have few enemies. Most animals quickly learn not to bother a skunk. But some animals will risk being sprayed in the hopes of catching a skunk. They include the Great Horned Owl, coyote, fox, badger and the fisher.

The owl has better luck than other animals at avoiding the skunk's smelly secret weapon. A Great Horned Owl can swoop down so swiftly and so silently that the skunk often does not know it is there until it is too late. Even the skunk's spray does not stop the owl. The smell does not seem to bother it at all.

Those black eyes are very nearsighted and can barely see objects eight metres (25 feet) away.

Getting Around

The Striped Skunk has a stocky body and short legs. When it walks, it waddles a bit like a duck. But if it has to, the skunk can run in a quick gallop and reach speeds up to 14 kilometres (9 miles) per hour. But because the skunk has small lungs, it tires quickly and can only keep that speed up for a short time.

Walking isn't the only way skunks get around. All skunks are fine swimmers and often dog-paddle across ponds. Perhaps when skunks swim in this way we should say they skunk-paddle.

All Striped Skunks have some white hair on their tails, if only on the tip.

Some skunks have very narrow stripes on their backs, but others--like this fellow--have very wide stripes.

A Coat that Warms and Warns

The skunk's two-layered fur coat helps keep it warm in cold weather. A thick inner layer of kinky fur acts much like sheep's wool to keep in body heat. An outer layer of extra-long guard hairs keeps out the cold and rain.

But the skunk's coat is useful for warning as well as warming. Those bold white stripes on black are easy to recognize. They let other animals know:"Stay away. If not, I might spray!"

Even a young skunk has 34 razor sharp teeth.

Snacking with Skunks

What do skunks eat? Everything and anything.

A skunk's favorite treats are insects—everything from beetles to grubs and grasshoppers. To find these insects, a skunk depends on its keen sense of smell. The skunk usually walks along with its sensitive nose to the ground. That way it can easily sniff out insects or other little creatures living underground or hiding in the grass. It will even sneeze several times on these walks to clear its nose and help it smell better.

If a skunk smells insects underground, it digs them out with its front feet. That job is easy because each front foot has five very long, strong claws. Skunks are also very fond of eggs and will dig out any turtle or snake eggs they can find.

Skunks do not always sleep during the day. If they are hungry they may start to feed at dusk or even in broad daylight.

The skunk has a very keen sense of hearing too. If it hears small creatures rustling in the grass, it will pounce on them. Mice, shrews, voles, birds, chipmunks, even cottontail rabbits are all prey for the skunk. Sometimes the skunk will feed on dead animals as well and if the skunk lives near a pond or marsh, it feasts on frogs, snakes, minnows, lizards and crayfish too.

Skunks also feed on berries, apples and other fruit, as well as grass, leaves and buds. Skunks that live in farm country often munch on grains, such as corn and barley. But even though skunks eat crops, most farmers like having skunks nearby. That's because the skunks eat up many of the insects and mice that often destroy farm crops.

Skunk paw prints

Night Feeders, Day Dreamers

Skunks eat at night. As soon as it gets dark, the skunk waddles quietly through its territory looking for food. The size of a skunk's territory depends on the amount of food in the area. If there is a lot of food, the territory will be small. If food is scarce, the territory will be much larger. Usually the skunk's home territory is about four hectares (10 acres).

Within its territory, the skunk makes a den to sleep in during the day. Although the skunk will sometimes dig out its own burrow, it usually takes over a den abandoned by another animal. Sometimes it sleeps in hollow tree stumps, woodpiles or under buildings. But whatever its home, the skunk always lines it with dried leaves and grasses to make a cozy nest.

The skunk does not store food in its den for winter munching. Instead it feasts so much in the fall that it builds up a thick layer of fat on its body.

Wintertime Skunks

Skunks in southern areas are active year round. In those areas, the weather stays mild, and the skunk is able to hunt and find food.

But the skunks living farther north settle down in dens to sleep through the cold weather.

Skunks do not hibernate like chipmunks and Ground Squirrels do. These true hibernators sleep all winter, but skunks wake up from time to time. In fact, a skunk will leave its den on mild winter nights to search for food. But once the weather turns cold again, it crawls back into its den for a few days more sleep.

A skunk usually dens up alone, but sometimes it will share a den with another skunk. Occasionally two or more whole families will snuggle up together.

Mating Time

Skunks mate during the warm spells of weather in late February or early March. To find a mate, a male skunk wanders through its territory, traveling several kilometres (miles) a night. Two males will sometimes fight over the same female skunk. But they rarely spray one another.

A male skunk often mates with several female skunks during the mating season. After a female skunk has mated, she may go back to her den to sleep some more.

A skunk is ready to mate by the time it reaches its first birthday.

Skunk Birthday

In early spring the female skunk gives birth to four to six babies in her grass-lined den. One mother skunk gave birth to 18 babies in the same litter. That's a record!

Newborn skunks are so tiny that you could easily hold two of them in the palm of your hand. They weigh barely 28 grams (1 ounce) each and measure just 10 centimetres (4 inches) from the tip of their noses to the end of their tails. They are born deaf and blind.

The newborn skunks have hardly any hair. But even so, the outline of black-and-white stripes shows faintly in their thin baby hair.

A young skunk stops drinking its mother's milk and starts eating insects when it is six weeks old.

Fast Growers

The baby skunk spends its early days in the den with its mother. When it is not sleeping, it is drinking its mother's milk. It grows quickly. At one week old, it has doubled its birth weight. By the time it is three weeks old, it is crawling around the den.

There is much play fighting in the den between the skunk brothers and sisters. When they are a month old, the young skunks practice lifting their tails as if they were about to spray. But nothing happens. They cannot spray their musk until they are about six or seven weeks old. That is when they leave the den and need their secret weapon.

A young skunk rarely travels alone until it is three months old.

Skunks on Parade

When the young skunk is ready to leave the den, it does not go out alone. Instead, the mother skunk leads it out with its brothers and sisters.

The mother skunk and her young family look like a little parade of black-and-white fur as they wander through the night. The mother skunk is very strict and does not let her young wander away by themselves. Instead, she leads the way, and the young follow close behind in a single file. This way the mother can keep a watchful eye on her babies and protect them from danger.

The young skunks are usually safe near their mother. To protect them, she would not hesitate to spray a predator or any creature that came too close to her family.

On these outings, the young skunks learn how to hunt and find food by watching their mother. She shows them how to dig for grubs and other insects. Soon the young are feasting on insects and sampling berries and tasty plants. And if they are lucky and fast enough, they might even catch a mouse.

Opposite page:

A skunk often stops to dig up a grub or two as it ambles along.

Leaving Home

As the young skunks grow bigger and stronger, they go on longer and longer outings with their mother each night. By the fall, however, the skunk family usually breaks up. The young skunks wander away to find dens of their own. Sometimes one or two of the young skunks will stay with their mother until the following spring. Then they too are ready to go off or by themselves and start families of their own.

How can you tell if a skunk has been digging in your lawn? There will be small cone-shaped holes in ground where it has been digging.

Man's Friends

Skunks' powerful and unpleasant smell is enough to make people stay away from them. But even though we might not be able to get too near a skunk we should be glad that they are around. Why? The skunk's appetite for insects helps control pests that might otherwise eat farmers' crops.

So next time you see a skunk waddling through the woods or even at the zoo, think twice about turning up your nose and saying ''Pheww.'' Remember—there is more to the skunk than its smell.

It has been said that skunks destroy more insects than all other mammals put together.

Special Words

Burrow   A hole dug by an animal to be used as a home.

Den   Animal home.

Desert   Hot, dry area with few plants or trees.

Gland   A part of an animal's body that makes and gives out a substance.

Guard hairs   Long, coarse hairs that make up the outer layer of the skunk's coat.

Hibernate   To go into a heavy sleep for the winter.

Litter   Group of animal brothers and sisters.

Mate   To come together to produce young.

Musk   A substance with a strong smell that lasts a long time.

Naturalist   A person who studies nature.

Predators   Animals that live by hunting others for food.

Prey   A meal for a predator.

Scrub   Poor land that grows only small stunted trees and bushes.

Territory   Area that an animal or group of animals lives in and often defends from animals of the same kind.

INDEX

Cover Photo: Norman Lightfoot (Eco-Art Productions)

Photo Credits: E. Degginger (Miller Services), page 4; Norman Lightfoot (Eco-Art Productions), pages 7, 40; Stephen J. Krasemann (Valan Photos), pages 8, 15, 42; Ontario Ministry of Natural Resources, page 11; Bill Ivy, pages 12, 19, 20, 24, 35, 37, 44, 46; Robert C. Simpson (Valan Photos), page 16; William Lowry (Lowry Photo), page 23; Bruno Kern, pages 26, 39; Michel Quintin (Valan Photos), page 28; Alfred Kuhnigk (Valan Photos), page 31; Barry Griffiths (Network Stock Photo File), page 32.